READING COMPREHENSION
UNIQUE STORIES

PAGE	TITLE	CONCEPTS AND SKILLS
1	Real or Not?	Facts, Vocabulary, Interpretation
2	America's Heritage	Reading Comprehension
3	America's Heritage continued	Categorization, Interpretation
4	A Floating Iceberg Did It!	Reading Comprehension
5	A Floating Iceberg continued	Facts, Opinion, Vocabulary, Research
6	Here Comes the Parade!	Reading Comprehension
7	Parade continued	Sequencing, Opinion, Creative Thinking
8	(Student's Choice)	Reading Comprehension
9	(Student's Choice) continued	Main Idea, Facts, Interpretation, Classification
10	Who Dunnit?	Reading Comprehension
11	Who Dunnit? continued	Facts, Interpretation, Opinion
12	Things a Collector Can't Live Without	Facts, Inference, Interpretation
13	Lights, Camera, Action!	Reading Comprehension
14	Lights, Camera, Action! continued	Vocabulary, Sequencing, Interpretation, Facts, Opinion
15	Who Knows?	Reading Comprehension
16	Who Knows? continued	Facts, Opinion, Interpretation
17	It Was a Challenge.	Reading Comprehension
18	Challenge continued	Facts, Interpretation, Vocabulary, Sequencing
19	At the End	Reading Comprehension
20	At the End continued	Facts, Vocabulary, Inference, Opinion

TEACHER'S GUIDE

The purpose of this book is to develop comprehension in reading through interesting and unique stories about a variety of subjects. The activities in this book provide practice in comprehension, opinion, sequencing, vocabulary, finding facts, and recall.

The focus of the book is to strengthen students' overall reading abilities and to refine the necessary reading skills so that students will enjoy reading to a greater degree.

Share and enjoy these stories and exercises with your students.

For additional supplementary reading material see:
READING COMPREHENSION — STRANGER THAN FICTION.
READING COMPREHENSION — MYSTERIES.
READING COMPREHENSION — SPORTS SHORTS.
READING COMPREHENSION — UNIQUE AMERICANS.

ANSWERS

Page 1
1. People have ordered works of art.
   Students copy works of art to learn from them.
   Criminals sell them as real works of art.
2. To make money or because he/she liked the piece of art.
3. dealer's personal knowledge, magnifying glass, trust in the source
4. age, finish, materials used
5. electric, chemical, temperature
6. Answers will vary. Accept reasonable answers.
   if paint used was not in existence at the time the real artist did the painting.
7. real, genuine, original, authentic
   fake, copy, imitation, forgery
8. a good artist
9. Accept reasonable answers.

Page 3

1.
EXPLORERS	SETTLERS
Columbus	John Smith
Coronado	William Penn
Marquette	Pilgrims
Daniel Boone	

SETTLEMENTS	TRANSPORTATION
Jamestown	Mayflower
Kentucky	covered wagons
Plymouth	
Pennsylvania	
California	

PATRIOTS	WARRIORS
Paul Revere	David Farragut
Patrick Henry	John Pershing
Alexander Hamilton	George Patton
Benjamin Franklin	Douglas MacArthur

PUBLIC OFFICIALS	PRESIDENTS
John Jay	Abraham Lincoln
Sam Rayburn	George Washington
William Seward	

MUSICIANS	ARTISTS
John P. Sousa	James Whistler
Stephen Foster	Gilbert Stuart

INVENTORS/ SCIENTISTS	OTHERS
Thomas Edison	Walt Disney
Alexander Graham Bell	Clara Barton
Samuel Morse	Paul Dunbar
	Horace Mann

2. He is still living.
3. They recognize the 300th anniversary of their settling.
4. 1847
5. George Washington and Benjamin Franklin

Page 5
1. proud, confident
2. Accept answers that will back-up student's first answer.
3. April 14, 1912
4. The ship was going too fast.
   The iceberg was seen too late.
   It was difficult to see.
5. There were not enough lifeboats.
6. was a festival of lights and music
7. rear - wire cage on a mast
   right side - raised platform across ship
8. calm, clear, still, cold, silent, etc.
9. Answers will vary.

Page 7
1.
F4	B7
P4	B2
F6	P3
B3	B5
P1	F1
B1	B4
F2	P2
P5	F3
F5	B6

2. creative, well-organized people
3. Answers will vary.
4. Answers will vary.

Page 9
1. Answers will vary.
2. insects
3. Its fossils remain in limestone.
4. Gallornis
5. ostrich
6. penguins
7. ostrich, rhea, cassowary, emu, kiwi
8. They hop onto trees and climb up.
9. Accept any reasonable answers.
10. They disappear.
11. They used them to swim, dive, and defend themselves.
12. Marrow makes bones heavier.

Page 11
1. Search for evidence.
   Look for stolen property.
   Look for victims and sunken objects.
   Rescue victims.
2. Z pattern, semicircular, parallel
3. When he spends a long time looking for something and finds nothing.
4. poor, visibility, strong currents, obstacles in water
5. Accept any reasonable answers.
6. Answers will vary.

Page 12
1. To receive pleasure from collections, for security or a secure feeling, to learn about a subject, etc.
2. Answers will vary.
3. Answers will vary.
4. A person might collect uniforms from the Civil War. Or, a person might collect buttons no matter when they were made. Accept reasonable answers.
5. What one man does not want, another does.

Page 14
1. precaution
   predict
   simulated
   execution
   careened
   feat
2. 2, 1, 4, 3
3. A person may be padded or an object hit could be padded.
   Props may be specially built or be light weight.
   Dummies and camera tricks may be used.
   Accept reasonable answers.
4. Accept reasonable answers.
5. He was replaced by a dummy.
6. talented, physically fit and healthy people
7. Accept reasonable answers.
8. Answers will vary.

Page 16
1. It has no moving parts and it is protected.
2. It controls speech, thinking, reflexes, movements, vision, memory, everything we do, hearing, etc.
3. They are not sure how it works or what area controls intelligence.
4. the same

5. It is a number. A ranking of how a person may perform.
6. from various tests
7. Accept reasonable answers.
8. Idiot is at the lower end of the intelligence scale. Savant is at the upper end.
9. It may be that an idiot savant's mind is less cluttered and he or she can concentrate more on one thing, or perhaps the whole brain is not retarded.
10. idiots
11. Accept all legible answers. There is no right or wrong amount of doubling of numbers. Compare students' answers to the case in the story.
12. Accept reasonable answers.

Page 18
1. 4, 2, 2
   2, 2
2. Christa McAuliffe was from there.
3. commander
   pilot
   launch a small platform to study Halley's comet
   study weightlessness and figure ways to build better satellites
   broadcast two lessons
4. Resnick, Onizuka, McNair
5. She was not a scientist nor a flier.
6. Astronauts train at Johnson Space Center. Space craft lift off from Cape Canaveral.
7. postponed, cancelled, scratched
8. Africa
9. 3
10. 4, 1, 5, 2, 6, 3

Page 20
1. True   True
   False   True
   True   False
   True   False
   False   True
   False   False
   True
2. suggestions, evidence, indications
3. deceased, lost one, corpses
4. rites
5. the end of a person's life
6. burning a dead body to ashes
7. - 9. Answers will vary.

Real or Not?

Works of art have been copied for centuries. Since ancient times people have ordered copies of sculptures, paintings, and metal work for their own pleasure and decoration. Besides copying a work of art because it is admired, students studying art copy pieces by original artists to learn and understand their techniques. There is nothing wrong with copying a work of art as long as it is not passed off as the real thing. If it is, it is a forgery. If it is sold as an original, it is dishonest.

Some forgeries are so good it is difficult to tell whether they are genuine or fake. Before the 1930's, there were no scientific methods to detect imitation works of art. An art dealer had to depend on his personal knowledge and a magnifying glass. He had to trust the source from whom a piece of art came if it did not come directly from the artist. Now there are ways of authenticating art. Temperature, electrical, and chemical tests can tell the age, kind of finish, and materials used in a work of art. Then it is possible to determine if it is a copy or authentic.

1. Why have there been forgeries of art? _______________________________________
____

2. Why would a person forge a work of art? _____________________________________
____

3. How was a real work of art determined 100 years ago? __________________________
____
____

4. What can tests determine? ____
5. What kind of tests are there? ____
6. Of what good is it to know what kind of paint was used? ________________________
____
____

7. List the words in the story that mean true. ___________________________________
____ false _______________________________
____

8. What would a good forger have to be? _______________________________________
9. What do you think buyers of original art should do before they make a purchase? ____
____

America's Heritage

These illustrations represent the commemorative stamps issued to honor these famous individuals.

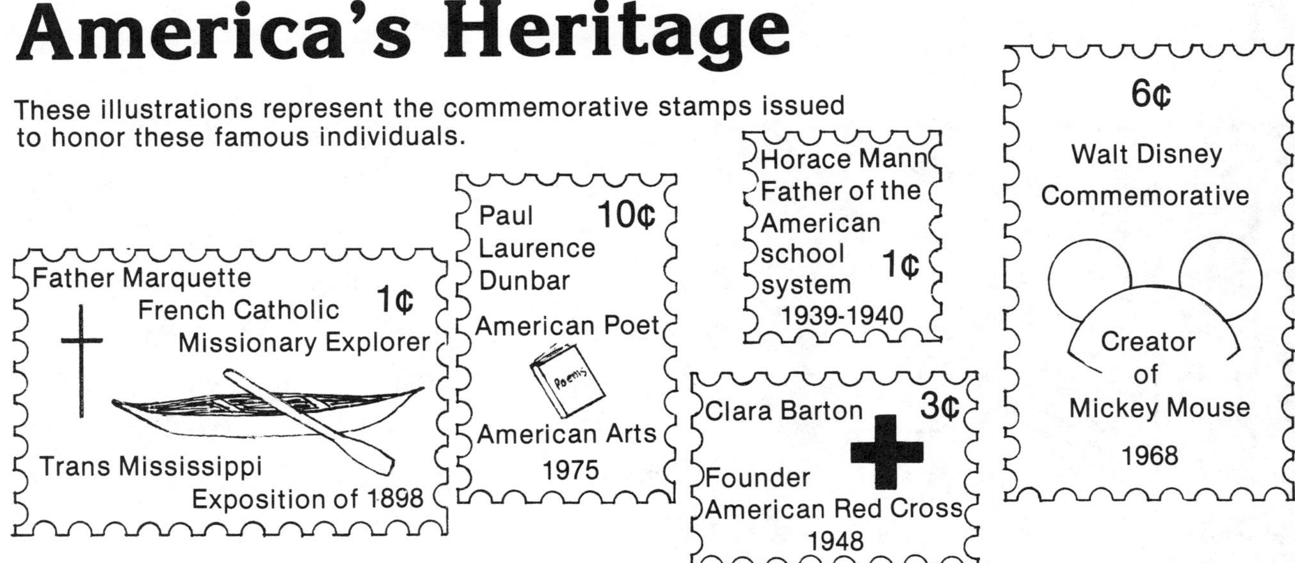

Many people have had a hand in building America. Some have done so because they were in search of a new world or a better way of life. Some have given of themselves to make America a better place in which to live. Others had a special talent which they shared with America and the world. Many of these people have been honored on commemorative stamps.

Commemoratives are special postage stamps that honor important people or events. It is a good way to learn America's history.

The first commemorative stamps were issued in 1893. They honored the discovery of the New World 400 years before with pictures of both Columbus and his fleet. Several explorers of America have been honored. Coronado, who searched the southwest in 1540, was honored on a three-cent stamp in 1940 for example. Once new lands had been discovered, they were settled. John Smith helped settle the first English settlement, Jamestown, in 1607. Pilgrims made the journey to the New World on the Mayflower and settled at Plymouth in 1620. Both settlements were honored on commemoratives in 1907 and 1920 respectively. William Penn escaped being imprisoned in England and settled his colony, Pennsylvania. Daniel Boone explored the inland wilderness. Settlers seeking adventure or more open land followed after him to settle in Kentucky and other inland territories. When gold was discovered in California, in 1848, people traveled across the country in covered wagons to seek their fortunes.

The United States issued its first stamps in 1847. Benjamin Franklin and George Washington were on them. Others who did so much during the early years of the nation are also pictured on stamps — Paul Revere, Patrick Henry, Alexander Hamilton. Battles in America's early years were led by able warriors like David Farragut, John Pershing, George Patton, and Douglas MacArthur.

America's Heritage continued

No living President has had his picture on a United States postage stamp. However, every deceased President has his picture on at least one. Some stamps honor public officials who were never elected as president such as John Jay, the first Supreme Court justice, William Seward, Lincoln's Secretary of State, and Sam Rayburn, Speaker of the House.

Without the genius of such inventors and scientists as Samuel Morse, Alexander Graham Bell, and Thomas Edison, different parts of the world may have lived isolated from one another. Musicians John Philip Sousa and Stephen Foster and artists Gilbert Stuart and James Whistler made the world a more pleasant place. Contributors to American literature and education, and women have been honored by having their pictures or causes on stamps.

1. Review the story and the illustrations on page 2. Complete the chart. Not all spaces will be filled.

	SETTLERS		TRANSPORTATION
Columbus		Jamestown	
	William Penn		

PATRIOTS		PUBLIC OFFICIALS	
	David Farragut		Abraham Lincoln

		INVENTORS/SCIENTISTS	OTHERS
John P. Sousa	Gilbert Stuart		

2. Why wouldn't Jimmy Carter be on a stamp? _______________________________________

3. Why were stamps issued honoring Jamestown in 1907 and Plymouth in 1920? _________

____

____

4. When were the first commemorative stamps issued? _______________________________

5. Whose pictures were on them? ____

A Floating Iceberg Did It!

The Titanic was a British steamer. It was the largest ship in the world and believed to be unsinkable. She was on her maiden voyage, her first sailing, from England to New York, in April, 1912. The ship moved steadily through the still water with its more than 2200 crew and passengers. The crew was proud of their ship. They did everthing they could to assure the passengers' comfort. The passengers were enjoying the beauty and luxury of the new ship and its services.

The ship was a festival of lights and music as it glided through the darkness on the fourteenth of April. The night air had a chill about it. Some passengers had retired to their beds where they could get warm under the covers. Others chose to keep warm in the public rooms dancing, playing cards, and talking with one another.

Two officers on the bridge kept their eyes on the sea ahead watching for icebergs. Two lookouts were watching from the crow's nest, a wire cage on a mast, about 100 feet above the water. It was difficult to see on that clear night because the sea was so calm. If the ocean had had movement, the lookouts could better see water breaking around the base of an iceberg even if they could not see the berg itself. But there seemed to be little to worry about on this great ship, and it moved speedily on course.

Suddenly, the lookouts broke the night's silence with shouts, "Iceberg straight ahead!" It was too late. The iceberg's lower ledge scraped half way along the starboard side of the Titanic and made an opening in it. The ship began to sink. There were not enough lifeboats. Women and children were placed in them first. The band kept playing to keep everyone calm. It was still playing two-and-a-half hours later when the Titanic's stern pointed almost straight up in the air. People jumped or were thrown into the water as the great ship slipped from sight beneath the water.

      READ. COMP.-UNIQUE STORIES

A Floating Iceberg continued

Lifeboats were able to pick up some of the people in the water. A few hours later, 705 survivors were rescued by another passenger ship, the Carpathia. The exact number of people who lost their lives is still unknown. The figures range between 1490 and 1517.

The exact location of the ship was also unknown until 1985, when French and American researchers found the wreckage. Later French divers found over 800 objects. Some belonged to the ship such as a statue of a cherub from the ship's grand staircase and a locked safe. Some objects were the personal belongings of the passengers. As incredible as it was for the researchers to discover the final resting place of the Titanic, it was a haunting experience to find where approximately 1500 people had lost their lives.

1. How did the crew feel about the Titanic? _______________________________

2. Why did they feel that way? _______________________________
____

3. What was the exact date of the Titanic's disaster? _______________________________

4. Check the reasons below you think the iceberg hit the Titanic.

____ The ship was going too fast.   ____ There were not enough lookouts.

____ The iceberg was seen too late.   ____ It was difficult to see.

____ There were too many passengers.   ____ The music was too loud.

5. Why were so many people lost? _______________________________

6. What phrase in the story makes the ship seem alive? _______________________________
____

7. What are the following parts of a ship?

stern _______________________   crow's nest _______________________

starboard _______________________   bridge _______________________

8. Write three adjectives that describe the night – before the accident. _______________________________
____

9. Describe the feelings you would have had and why for the following situations.

If I had been in a lifeboat I would have felt _______________________________
____

If I had been the lookout on the crow's nest I would have felt _______________________________
____

If I had been the band leader I would have felt _______________________________
____

Here Comes the Parade!

Many parades have become traditional. Every Thanksgiving, Macy's Department Store has a huge parade in New York City. On New Year's Day, the Tournament of Roses parade precedes the Rosebowl football game in Pasadena, California. In February, New Orlean's Mardi Gras parade attracts people from all over. On July 4th, many American towns, large and small, have parades with waving flags and marching bands. Everyone loves a parade — marchers and spectators alike. Television brings major parades into the homes of people who cannot go to the parades. What onlookers see in big parades has probably taken over a year to produce.

Behind every parade is one person in charge. The director is backed up by several assistants and committees. One of the first tasks is choosing a theme if there is to be one. Finding a Grand Marshal to lead the parade is next. A Grand Marshal is usually a well-known celebrity who will attract a crowd. Bands who have been reviewed and who wish to participate in a parade, send letters telling of their desire. Invitations to the top bands are sent so they will have time to earn the money necessary to make the trip to the parade's city. If there is a theme, notices are sent to prospective participants so they can begin to plan their floats and costumes. Designers get started immediately on their sponsor's entry into the parade. They must follow regulations set by the parade officials.

Have you ever wondered what goes into making the floats or huge balloons for parades? The Tournament of Roses requires an entire float be covered with something that grows. Floats for other parades may use other coverings. The most important part of all floats is their understructure. Carpenters first build a form close to the final shape over the vehicle that will carry the float. Welders secure the form with supporting rods and add other parts to give it shape. Any mechanical parts are put into position by electricians and engineers before a wire netting is cut, pulled, and tacked over the form carefully to keep its shape. The wire is then covered with a plastic spray to fill in spaces in the netting.

Two days before the Tournament of Roses parade the flowers begin to be attached by teams working day and night. Each flower is placed in a small tube

Parade continued

filled with water and a special chemical to keep it fresh and then pushed through the netting. Or flower petals are pasted on the float with glue that has a preservative in it. Some floats have used over 300,000 flowers. Floats for other parades may be completed with papier mâché and/or plastic rather than fresh materials.

Balloon makers begin with an idea. They draw how it should look. Then they make a wax model. Detailed drawings are made, enlarged to the desired size, and used as patterns. A rubberized fabric is cut from the patterns. The different pieces are glued together with rubber cement. The balloons are so big that they consist of several compartments. Each compartment is filled with helium and painted with a special paint. When the paint is dry, the balloon is deflated and kept in a box until the night before the parade. Balloons are expensive and take a lot of work to make, but they may be used more than once.

Finally, it is time for the parade to begin. The Grand Marshal moves out, followed by a year or two of hard work. Viewers are entertained for an hour or two, and then it is over — until the next time!

1. Identify each activity below as a step to preparing for a parade (**P**), building a float (**F**), or making a balloon (**B**). Then number each activity in order in each category (**P1, P2,** etc.).

   ____ Wire netting cut, pulled, tacked in place.
   ____ Participants told of theme and regulations.
   ____ Final material placed on it.
   ____ Wax model made.
   ____ Theme selected.
   ____ It begins with an idea.
   ____ Welders secure and make shape more identifiable.
   ____ Designers begin planning floats and costumes.
   ____ Plastic spray covers netting.
   ____ Painted with special paint.
   ____ Drawings made of idea.
   ____ Top bands invited to participate.
   ____ Rubberized fabric cut along pattern lines.
   ____ Carpenters build frame over vehicle that will carry float.
   ____ Detailed drawings made and enlarged.
   ____ Grand Marshal chosen.
   ____ Mechanical parts put into position.
   ____ Pieces glued together.

2. What kind of people help produce a parade? _______________________________________

3. Think of a theme for a parade. What is it? _______________________________________

4. Draw a float or a balloon for your parade on the back of this page.

____

Scientists believe that between 150 and 135 million years ago there were some insect-eating, lizardlike reptiles that hopped on their hind legs. One day one of these creatures hopped up into a tree. It discovered it was safe from its enemies and that there was plenty of food to be found in the tree. This creature was joined by others of its kind. Gradually, over millions of years their scales turned into feathers and their forearms became wings. They developed into birds. Scientists called these creatures *Proavis*, the Latin word for prebird.

The earliest bird known was the *Archaeopteryx* (är′kē ahp tə riks) about 135 million years ago. They remain as fossils in limestone. It took many years for birds to change from the heavy and awkward Archaeopteryx to lighter birds that could fly up into the air. About 120 million years ago, a wading bird with hollow bones evolved called *Gallornis*. It may be an ancestor to the flamingo. Birds are well designed for life in the air. During the millions of years it took for birds to evolve, they developed features that would best serve them in flight.

After evolving as birds, some creatures lost their ability to fly because of their needs. It took as long for them to change back to nonflying birds as it had for them to evolve into flying ones. There are forty-nine flightless birds.

Flat-breasted runners have no need to fly. They no longer have strong flight muscles or the keel-shaped breastbone most flying birds have. Their flight feathers are fluffy like down. They have stong, heavy legs from four to eight feet tall. Their leg bones are partially filled with marrow. The ostrich is the largest of this group. In fact, it is the largest living bird. Other birds in this group are the rhea, cassowary, emu, and kiwi.

Twenty-two kinds of birds, fifteen of which are penguins, have adapted to life in water. Other water birds are grebes, ducks, and one type of cormorant. Because these birds use their wings for swimming, diving, and defending themselves, they have kept the keel-shaped breastbone and strong breast

_______________________________ continued

muscles usually used for flying.

Rails are a family of birds. The family once had 132 species. Only seven of the flightless kind remain. They have small rounded wings and short, soft tails. They live on warm islands in the South Pacific. They scurry about the ground looking for food. Some of them can swim and run when necessary.

When we see a bird sitting on a branch of a tree, we assume it flew there. In most cases it did. But there are six birds with feet that can climb to their perch. These birds can leap a few feet off the ground with flapping wings, but they cannot fly.

Some birds have evolved back to where they began. They live in an environment that provides all they need and they have no enemies to fear. Do you think they will survive without being able to fly?

1. Write what you think would be a good title for this story on the line at its beginning and at the top of this page.

2. What did prebirds eat? ____

3. How do we know what the first bird was like? ___________________________

   ____

4. What may have been the flamingo's ancestor? ___________________________

5. What is the world's largest bird? ______________________________________

6. What is the largest group of water birds? _____________________________

7. What birds belong to the flat-breasted runner's group? _________________

   ____

8. How do birds that do not fly get into trees? __________________________

   ____

9. Do you think the rail family will ever be extinct? ________ Explain your answer. ______

   ____

10. What happens to the flight features of birds when they no longer fly? __________

   ____

11. Why did the water birds keep their stong breast muscles? _______________

   ____

12. What does marrow in the bones of birds do to their weight? _____________

   ____

Who Dunnit?

Not many crimes remain unsolved today because the evidence is thrown into the water! Several police departments have their own diving teams. Those too small to have their own team borrow from the nearest police department that has one.

Police divers not only search for evidence, they also recover stolen property, and victims and vehicles of plane, car, or boating accidents. Most work is scheduled. Some is emergency work. Skaters falling through thin ice or cars driving into the water with passengers constitute emergency situations. If a passenger is trapped in a car and not rescued within five minutes, the chance of survival is slim. A diving team's work is not always in a river or lake. It may be in deep rock quarries or canals.

Underwater searches are slow. The teams want to be sure an area is thoroughly covered. There are various types of search patterns. They may be one diver moving in a **Z** or semicircular pattern. A parallel search pattern is two divers holding onto either side of a net being dragged behind a boat with one hand while the other hand feels for the object.

Some days are more successful than others. Sometimes divers find the object they are looking for. Sometimes they don't, but they may find several other items. These are turned in and checked to see if they have been reported missing or have been used in a crime. Sometimes divers spend days looking for one piece of evidence. They can become discouraged, but when they find what they are looking for, their spirits are raised.

Underwater searches can have problems. Visibility is usually poor, and seeing is more difficult. Brightly colored plastic lines make it easier for the divers to stay in the search area. Underwater currents may be stong. They may carry objects away from their pinpointed location or they may sweep the diver away from the search area. Divers may have to contend with obstacles such as huge rocks, uneven terrain, or foreign objects thrown into the water. Even some underwater animal life can be dangerous. Divers must be careful that they do not become entangled in an underwater maze and that nothing falls on them.

Who Dunnit? continued

Being a police diver is challenging. It is rewarding when what is being sought is found. A diver's findings can be unexpected. One day a police boat going under a bridge met with a tremendous splash. A body had hit the water just beside the boat. A diver pulled it from the water and saved one person's life. A diver's findings may seem unusual. One diver swam into a circus cage. Another found forty cars while looking for one. Other unexpected items found beneath the surface include false teeth, lawn mowers, office machines, horse trailers, and explosives. Finding unusual items is usual for divers.

1. Name four duties of a diving team. ______________________________________

   ____

   ____

   ____

2. Name three search patterns. ____

   ____

   ____

3. Why might a diver become discouraged? __________________________________

   ____

4. What are three problems divers could have?

   ____

   ____

   ____

5. How could each one affect the diver's work? ______________________________

   ____

   ____

   ____

6. Would you want to be a police diver? ___________ Why or why not? ___________

   ____

   ____

Things a Collector Can't Live Without

A collector is a collector is a collector! People like to collect things. Perhaps it gives them pleasure, a chance to learn about a specific subject, or a sense of security. Whatever the reasons, once a person is "bitten" by the collecting bug, he or she wants to collect as much as possible of that particular thing — or maybe as much as possible of many things!

One wonders what makes people want to collect the things they do. Some collect items made only of one material like tin, paper, or wood. Some collections are from a specific period of time. Others are one specific item from over a long period of time. Some unique collectables are electric light bulbs, dental equipment, sugar wrappers, hair brushes, cannons, egg cups, nails, and gloves.

Some collectable items are valuable. Others are just fun to have, but not worth a lot. There is a saying that goes, "One man's trash is another man's treasure." There is always something for someone and someone for that thing.

1. What is the reason people collect things? _______________________

____

2. Where are some places a collector would look to find the following?

electric light bulbs _______________________ sugar wrappers _______________________

gloves _______________________ cannons _______________________

dental equipment _______________________ nails _______________________

hair brushes _______________________ egg cups _______________________

3. What sort of items might be in a paper collection? _______________________

____

4. Explain the difference between collecting items from a specific time and collecting a specific item over a long period of time. Give examples.

____

____

____

5. Explain the saying "One man's trash is another man's treasure." _______________________

____

Lights, Camera, Action!

There are 200 stunt men and women in movies and television. Stunt artists fill in or double for actors when the going gets rough. When a script calls for dangerous action, a stunt person reads what is called for, plans its execution, practices it many times, and finally performs it in place of the actor. Stunt artists do not consider themselves superpeople. They know there is some risk in their work and that accidents do occur. They accept the danger as part of the job description, but they take every precaution. They do not accept parts that require impossible and amazing feats. They do not want to be heroes - just stunt men and women. Stunt people refer to their stunts as "gags." There are many gags performed in movies and on television. Invisible prop and camera techniques and the acrobatics of the stunt people make it possible to make the scenes look real.

A car sped down the street, careened around a corner, jumped a curb, went through a fence, and came to the end of its run when it exploded against a brick wall. How do they do it? There are many "tricks" to such simulated scenes in movies and television.

Cars used in chases are specially outfitted to protect the drivers. Drivers usually wear padding. Chases through real city streets often need the cooperation of the local police. In a car chase where a car goes over the cliff, the stunt person stops the car at the edge of the cliff and is replaced by a dummy before the fatal fall.

Stunt doubles rarely hit one another in a fight. The camera makes the viewer think they do. "Good guys" running after "bad guys" is like a car chase. It takes a lot of planning and practice. Pads protect a stunt person when he falls, but that person must also know how to fall. When a stunt person jumps from a high place, the fall is cushioned. Boxes fastened together, piled high, and filled with air and mattresses are often-used props for breaking a fall. Helicopter rescue scenes are common. Sometimes when a copter lifts a heavy object like

Lights, Camera, Action! continued

a car into the air, the object is made of plastic. Water "gags" are difficult to plan because the water's pressure and current are hard to predict. Fire stunts are dangerous. Safety persons always stand by with fire extinguishers.

Many stunt artists are former athletes, circus and rodeo performers, or they were taught by their stunt-artist parents. Stunt artists must be skilled physically and must stay in good physical shape. Though they do not take chances, they want the stunts to look exciting and believable. Next time you see a dangerous situation on film ask, "How was it done?"

1. Write the words from the story that fit the definitions below.

    _____________________ a measure taken to prevent harm

    _____________________ ability to foresee what will happen

    _____________________ made to look real

    _____________________ the process of carrying out an act

    _____________________ leaned over to one side

    _____________________ an act of courage

2. Number the sentences below in order to tell what goes into performing a gag.

    ____ Stunt person plans how he or she will do stunt.

    ____ Stunt person studies what is to be done.

    ____ The stunt is practiced many times.

    ____ Necessary precautions are built-in.

3. What are some of the "tricks" used to create dangerous scenes on film? _________

    ____

    ____

    ____

4. How could local police be helpful planning a chase on city streets? ___________

    ____

5. What do you think happened to the driver in the simulated scene in the story? ______

    ____

6. Who make good stunt artists? ______________________________________

    ____

7. How do you think the following situations are accomplished?

    a car hitting a rock wall ____

    a man falling from an airplane _______________________________________

    a boat surviving a broken dam _______________________________________

    a man trapped in a fire ____

8. On the back of this page, describe your favorite "action" scene from a movie.

Who Knows?

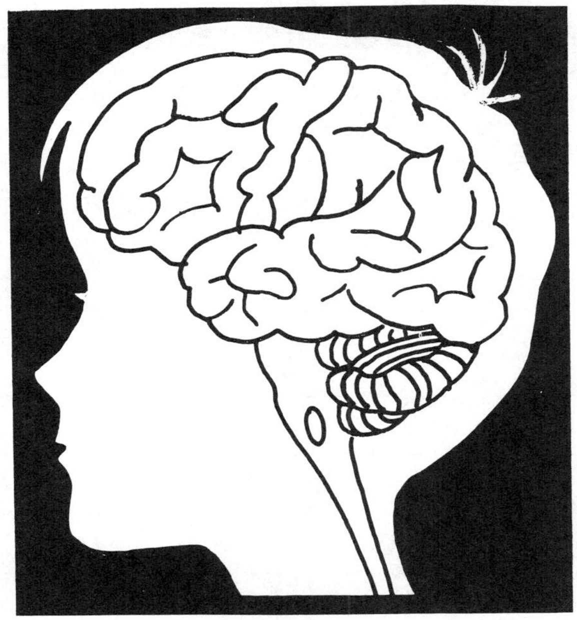

One organ in your body needs less care than any other. It has no moving parts and is protected by its own casing. This organ, the brain, is responsible for everything you do. It controls your speech, thinking, uncontrolled reflexes like blinking, and controlled movements like walking. No one is sure how it works. Scientists have learned that certain areas of the brain control specific actions such as speech, vision, memory, and swallowing. Though intelligence can be measured, scientists are not sure which area controls it. They have looked at the brains of geniuses next to those with more limited power, and to the naked eye, there is no difference.

A person's intelligence quotient, or I.Q., may be measured on individual (usually oral) or group (usually written) tests. The results of such a test is a number. Average intelligence ranges between 90-110. More than forty percent of the population has an average I.Q. About one percent of the population is above 140 and about three percent is below 70. An I.Q. should not be considered the only measure of a person's intelligence, but it can be an indicator of what a person is capable of doing.

An idiot's I.Q. is in the lowest range of scores. A savant is a person with a great deal of knowledge. Therefore, the term "idiot savant" is contradictory with the definitions of idiot and savant. Usually an idiot savant is mentally slow, but an idiot savant may be a genius in one specific area. There are known cases of idiot savants. One was a person who could barely do basic arithmetic, but could double numbers with the speed of a computer. Another was a person with an I.Q. below 40 who had an amazing talent for sketching. A third example is a spastic, blind, retarded boy who could play classical music by ear on the piano.

It is difficult to explain the idiot savant occurance. Scientists feel it may be that their minds are not as cluttered as the minds of those of average intelligence. Therefore, they can concentrate on one area without interruption.

Who Knows? continued

Perhaps mental retardation does not affect the entire brain and, therefore, leaves a part or parts of the brain to develop to its greatest capacity.

1. Why does the brain require less attention than other body organs? ___________
   ____

2. What are some things scientists know about the brain? ______________________
   ____
   ____

3. What don't they know about the brain? ___________________________________
   ____

4. How does the brain of a genius look next to the brain of an idiot? ______________

5. What is intelligence quotient? ____
   ____

6. How is it determined? ____

7. In your opinion what else should be an indicator of a person's intelligence? _______
   ____

8. Why is the term "idiot savant" contradictory? _____________________________
   ____

9. How is it explained by some? ____
   ____
   ____

10. Are there more geniuses or idiots? ______________________________________

11. Start with 3. Write the numbers doubling them. How far can you go in one minute? A
    computer could get up in the thousands. Can you?
    3, ____
    ____
    ____

12. Do you think talent and creativity are the same as intelligence? ________________
    Explain the reason for your answer. ____________________________________
    ____
    ____

It Was a Challenge.

On January 28, 1986, the space shuttle, Challenger, was scheduled to blast off. At Cape Canaveral, thousands of people with binoculars gathered on the ground to watch it rise into space. In Concord, New Hampshire, students filled the high school auditorium to watch the shuttle launch on television. They watched because a social studies teacher from Concord, Christa McAuliffe, had been selected from the applications of over 11,000 educators to be the first private citizen to fly into space. She was to broadcast two lessons to American students from space.

Christa McAuliffe was one of seven crew members. The others were experienced pilots and skilled scientists. The commander of the flight was Francis "Dick" Scobee. He was an experienced flier. As a pilot he had flown over 6500 hours. He had flown on a Challenger previously. The pilot of the Challenger was Michael Smith. As a navy commander he had flown in combat, but he had never been in space. Dr. Judith Resnick was an electrical engineer. She had been in space before and was one of this mission's specialists. Another mission specialist was Dr. Ronald McNair, a laser physicist. He had been in space in 1984. Dr. McNair was going to launch a small science platform to study Halley's comet on the trip. Air Force Lieutenant Colonel Ellison Onizuka had been in space before. He was an aerospace engineer and the third mission specialist. Gregory Jarvis, a Hughes Aircraft Company engineer, planned to study weightless liquids, and figure out better ways to build satellites.

After training at the Johnson Space Center in Houston, Texas, the crew was flown to Cape Canaveral for the liftoff on January 25th. The flight was first postponed because of poor weather conditions at an emergency landing strip in Africa. The flight was cancelled a second time because weather forecasts for Florida were bad. The third launch was scratched because of high winds.

Finally, on January 28th the air was cool, but clear. The word was "GO." The seven astronauts suited up, filed onto the shuttle, and strapped themselves

Challenge continued

into their seats. The countdown began at 11:38 A.M. Mission Control began, "T minus 10,9,8,7,6, we have a main engine start, 4,3,2,1, liftoff." The ship rose quickly followed by trails of smoke. Mission Control instructed, "Challenger, go with throttle up." The pilot responded, "Roger, go with throttle up." Those were the last words from the Challenger.

The cheering that had filled the bleachers at Cape Canaveral and the seats in the auditorium in Concord, New Hampshire, came to an abrupt stop. Their eyes saw the horror. Challenger had exploded. The cheers turned to tears. Seventy-four seconds after the shuttle left the ground, it was over. The flight and the seven astronauts became history.

1. How many of the astronauts on the Challenger flight had been in space before? _______ were fliers? _______ were scientists? _______ were women? _______ were in one of the armed forces? _______

2. Why were the people of Concord, New Hampshire, especially interested in the flight of Challenger? ____

3. What were the specific duties of the following astronauts on this flight?
   Francis Scobee ____
   Michael Smith ____
   Ronald McNair ____
   Gregory Jarvis ____
   Christa McAullife ____

4. Who were the flight specialists? ____

5. Besides being a private citizen how was Christa McAullife different from the other astronauts? ____

6. What is the difference between the Johnson Space Center and Cape Canaveral?

   ____

   ____

7. What three words mean delay in the story? ____

8. Where could the shuttle land in an emergency? ____

9. How many delays were there before this flight could liftoff? _______________________

10. Number the following events in the order they occured.
    _____ flown to Cape Canaveral
    _____ applied to be first private citizen in space
    _____ waited at Cape Canaveral for liftoff
    _____ selected as first private citizen in space
    _____ January 28, 1986
    _____ trained at Johnson Space Center

At the End

Ceremonies have long accompanied the expiration of man. Since the beginning, death has been treated with love, respect, sorrow, denial, a sense of mystery, and even cannibalism. Rites associated with death are well established though they have been observed in many ways in different parts of the world over thousands of years.

There is evidence that very early man may have eaten his dead. Perhaps food was scarce. Perhaps it was thought that eating the flesh of the deceased gave some magical power to the living. It may have been a sign of respect. It may have been a way of keeping one's lost one closer to those that lived on. Why man may have performed this cannibalistic act remains unanswered.

Not all early burials were so gruesome. There are suggestions that Neanderthal Man buried his dead in shallow graves under the floors of the caves in which he lived. This may have been an attempt to keep lost ones close by to remain a part of the family.

As civilization changed, so did its burial customs. Shallow graves were replaced with deep pits or underground chambers. The body was placed there along with flowers, food, gifts, and some of the deceased's belongings. The living not only gave their time to preparing the departed's resting place and their personal treasures, but sometimes they gave their lives. There are indications that human sacrifices were made. Man and animal remains have been found in ancient graves. Some think the living gave their lives in order to serve their master or mistress in afterlife. Later, tombs above the ground appeared. The greatest of these were the pyramids of Egypt.

In most cultures, there is a solemn ceremony to send the dead off to the grave. America is no exception. It appears in America that the rites are not filled with as much emotion or tradition as in other parts of the world, but America does pay respect to its departed. They do not bury corpses with their belongings, servants, or food, but they are usually dressed in favorite clothes and may wear some jewelry. Whether a body is buried in the ground, in a tomb,

At the End continued

or cremated may be determined by the amount of money available and the beliefs of the deceased's family. Rich, poor, known, or unknown receive some kind of recognition at the end.

1. Write true or false in front of the following statements.

   ___________ There are several ways a dead body may be disposed of today.

   ___________ Americans do not choose to recognize death.

   ___________ There are many emotions connected with death.

   ___________ The way some dead were buried long ago was uncivilized.

   ___________ The Egyptians had the finest system of underground burial chambers.

   ___________ All burials in the beginning were uncivilized.

   ___________ Some early graves were dug in the floors of a family's home.

   ___________ Ancient people probably believed in an afterlife.

   ___________ Cannibalism is eating the flesh of another human being.

   ___________ People worldwide observe death in the same way.

   ___________ Burial customs have remained the same since the beginning.

   ___________ A person may be buried above or under the ground.

   ___________ Early man was cannibalistic because he was hungry.

2. There are three words used in the story that mean a clue or hint. What are they?

   ____

3. What words are used that refer to the dead person? ___________________________

   ____

4. What is the synonym used for ceremonies? ___________________________________

5. What does expiration mean in the story? ____________________________________

6. What is cremation? ____

7. Name three things that may have been buried in ancient times with a

   king or queen. ____

   caveman. ____

   warrior. ____

8. Why do you think some people have wanted to keep the body of the deceased close to

   them? ____

   ____

9. If we followed the customs of earlier times and other cultures, what items of value do

   you think would be buried with someone today? _______________________________